The Compulsion Cloud

WRITTEN BY
AVERI RIDGE CASTANEDA

ILLUSTRATED BY
VICKY KUHN

First published in Great Britain 2023 by Cherish Editions
Cherish Editions is a trading style of Shaw Callaghan Ltd
& Shaw Callaghan 23 USA, INC.
The Foundation Centre
Navigation House, 48 Millgate, Newark
Nottinghamshire NG24 4TS UK
www.triggerhub.org

British Library Cataloguing in Publication Data

A CIP catalogue record for this book is available upon request
from the British Library
ISBN: 978-1-915680-04-4

This book is also available in the following eBook formats:
ePUB: 978-1-915680-05-1

Averi Ridge Castaneda has asserted her right under the Copyright, Design and Patents Act 1988 to be identified as the author of this work

Illustrations by Vicky Kuhn Illustration
Cover design by Kathryn Davies
Typeset by Kathryn Davies

Cherish Editions encourages diversity and different viewpoints. However, all views, thoughts and opinions expressed in this book are the author's own and are not necessarily representative of us as an organization.

All material in this book is set out in good faith for general guidance and no liability can be accepted for loss or expense incurred in following the information given. In particular this book is not intended to replace expert medical or psychiatric advice. It is intended for informational purposes only and for your own personal use and guidance. It is not intended to act as a substitute for professional medical advice. Professional advice should be sought if desired before embarking on any health-related program.

ABOUT US

Cherish Editions is a bespoke author-funded publishing service for mental health, well-being and inspirational books. As a division of the TriggerHub Group, the UK's leading independent mental health and well-being organization, we are experienced in creating and selling positive, responsible, important and inspirational pieces of bibliotherapy, which work to de-stigmatize the issues around mental health and improve the well-being of those who read our titles. Cherish Editions is unique in that a percentage of the profits from the sale of our books goes directly to leading mental health charity Shawmind, to deliver its vision to provide support for those experiencing mental ill health.

Find out more about Cherish Editions by visiting cherisheditions.com or by joining us on:
Twitter @cherisheditions
Facebook @cherisheditions
Instagram @cherisheditions

Find out more about the work Shawmind do by visiting shawmind.org or by joining them on:
Twitter @Shawmind—
Facebook @ShawmindUK
Instagram @Shawmind—

To all of the children out there struggling with OCD, just remember,
you may have OCD, but OCD does not have you. I know you can and
WILL gain your power back. I believe in you!

~

I have so many people to thank for making this book come to life, but I
will keep this short and sweet! First, a big thank you to my husband Marvin
for always pushing me to follow my dreams and take a risk. This book may
not have happened without that extra push. Thank you to my mother and
father for always supporting me and reminding me to keep God at the
center of all things; He is the reason I am where I am today. Thank you
to my therapist who helped me understand what a big bully OCD is and
how to gain my power back. Most of all, thank you to the whole Cherish
Editions publishing team for giving me the opportunity to publish
The Compulsion Cloud. I will forever be grateful!

- Averi Ridge Castaneda

Holly walked into Ms. Anna's therapy office for the very first time. Holly was nervous, but Ms. Anna was very welcoming and made her feel comfortable.

Ms. Anna asked Holly,
"How are you feeling?
What has brought you
in to see me today?"

Holly paused for a moment, but she knew
she could trust Ms. Anna. So, she told her,

"A scary cloud is following me around.

It fills my head with anxious thoughts."

She went on, "The cloud tells me to do certain things. And if I don't do what it tells me, I feel very scared and nervous."

"If I do what it says," Holly continued, "it leaves me alone for a little while . . .

. . . But it always shows up again."

Holly told Ms. Anna that she only felt relief in the small amount of time when the cloud was gone.

The cloud would tell Holly to do certain things like . . .

"Tap your finger on your leg three times, or else something bad will happen to your mom and dad."

"Wash your hands three times, or else you will get sick and throw up."

"Check three times to make sure the stove is off before leaving home, or else your house will burn down."

And many other things.

Holly felt very nervous every time the cloud
urged her to do something.

She did not want anything bad to happen
to her family, her home or herself, so she
continued to do what the cloud told her.

But Holly told Ms. Anna,
"I don't want to feel anxious
and scared anymore.

I just want this cloud
to leave me alone!"

And yet, the cloud was constantly showing back up, even after Holly did what it told her to do. Because of this, she said, "I always feel exhausted, and my mind never shuts off."

Ms. Anna listened while Holly talked to her and shared how she was feeling. Luckily for Holly, Ms. Anna knew how she could get rid of the cloud.

She said, "The only way to make it go away is to give it less power. You have to face your fears and do the opposite of what the cloud tells you. It's time to start imagining the cloud as a big bully who constantly follows you around."

Ms. Anna then told Holly, "This cloud you're describing sounds a lot like a mental health condition called obsessive compulsive disorder. Most people call it OCD."

Holly asked Ms. Anna to please explain the disorder so she could understand more.

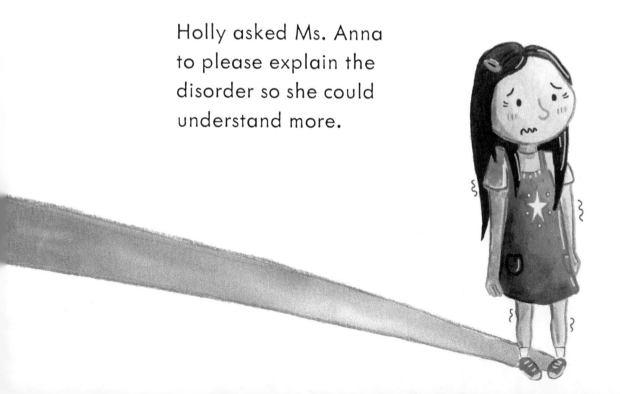

Ms. Anna said, "OCD is a disorder where you have recurring thoughts, called obsessions, that force you to perform certain actions, known as compulsions, over and over again until you feel relief.

People may see these behaviors as 'odd,' and because they don't understand OCD, they don't know how to help you. So, you get stuck in a cycle, meaning you will only feel relief for a small amount of time before you have another obsession or compulsion. The cloud that follows you is a compulsion cloud."

Holly paused.
"Yes! That is exactly what it feels like!
It's a really hard cycle to break out of, but
I want it to end. How do I make it stop?"

"Well," Ms. Anna said, "Exposure
and Response Prevention Therapy is
proven to help OCD. It is there to
encourage you to face your fears and stand
up to what this cloud is telling you to do.

You want to do the opposite of what the cloud is telling you. This may cause you a lot of anxiety at first, but over time, it will get easier, and the cloud will lose its power.

How about you try it this week at home?"

"I will try, but what happens if I can't stand up to the cloud? What happens if I feel too anxious? I already feel anxious now just thinking about it!" Holly said.

"It's normal to feel this way, and it's okay to not get it right the first time. Just remember to take baby steps and use coping skills to help you along the way."

Holly gave Ms. Anna
a very big smile.
"Thank you, I will
try that!"

The next morning, Holly was getting ready to eat breakfast before school and went to wash her hands. Then, the cloud that constantly followed her around spoke.

It ordered, "Wash your hands three times, or else you will get sick and throw up."

Holly washed her hands once and reached for the soap again, but then she remembered what Ms. Anna told her: "Do the opposite of what the cloud is telling you."

Holly could feel herself getting anxious, but she used her breathing techniques to calm herself down, then ate breakfast and went to school for the day.

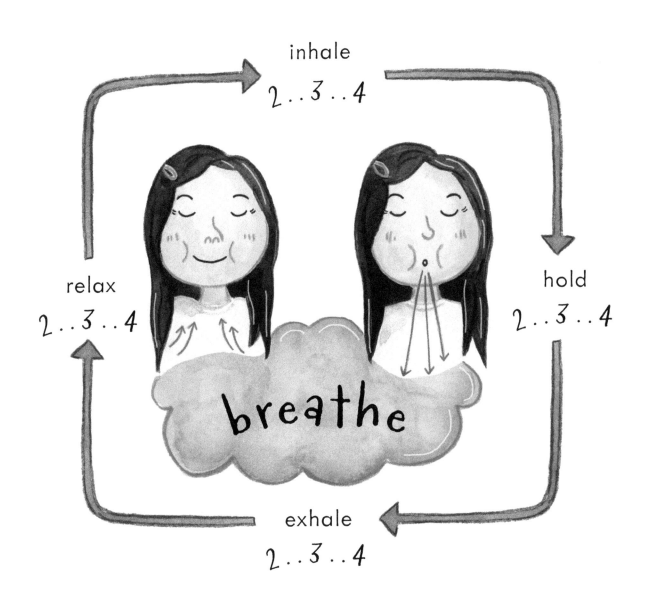

inhale
2..3..4

hold
2..3..4

exhale
2..3..4

relax
2..3..4

breathe

Holly struggled all day at school, worrying she would get sick since she only washed her hands once, not three times like she always did.

By the evening, though, Holly began to feel better. She didn't get sick. She didn't throw up. Nothing happened! Holly felt calm for once.

What the cloud told her wasn't true, which meant everything else it had told her had not been true, either. As she had this realization, Holly could feel the cloud shrinking above her, until —

POOF!

It was gone. Holly realized in that moment how much joy the cloud had taken from her, and she told herself, "Never again."

Holly took back her power that day, and many of you can, too.

OCD is a serious mental health disorder that affects more individuals than you think. Some people can have it more severely than others, but regardless, it is a condition that can interfere with daily functioning if left untreated.

If you or a loved one are experiencing something similar to the signs and symptoms described in this book, I would encourage you to seek out professional help and support, so you can take your power back, just like Holly did!

Printed in the USA
CPSIA information can be obtained
at www.ICGtesting.com
LVHW071350150324
774455LV00015B/159